SHADES
Of
Emotions

TIKIA CLEMENT

SHADES

Of
Emotions

About the Author

TIKIA CLEMENT is an author, poet, and songwriter from the Bronx, New York. She began writing at the age of seven because of her love for music. Tikia found comfort in writing music and poetry in the bathroom. Writing in the bathroom became a part of her process in creating music and poetry. She took time away from writing to further her education in Human Resource Management. She has an M.S. in Business Administration with a concentration in Human Resource Management.

In 2021, Ms. Clement self-published her first poetry book, "Eye Am Poetry." In 2023, she released "Testifying My Way," her poetic dedication to The Most High. 2024 and 2025 will be exciting for Tikia, as she will release a children's book, her third poetry book and a novel.

SHADES
Of
Emotions

TIKIA CLEMENT

Title: Shades of Emotions/Tikia Clement

Identifiers: **LCCN: 2024910751**
ISBN: **979-8-9908227-0-2 (paperback)**

Any references to historical events, real people, or real places are used fictitiously. Names, characters, and places are products of the author's imagination.

Published and Printed in the USA

First Printing Edition **2024.**
Publisher: **Dream Elite Strive for Xcellence Publishing**

Table of contents

SHADES
Of
Emotions

LIFE

Journey

Join me on this journey.
Walk in my shoes.
Try crossing those Manhattan streets during rush hour while the streetlights are green.
Look at me.
See my pain.
Can you tell?
I am accustomed to wearing it well.
Understand my hurt and despair.
I wake up most mornings with fear of not returning home.
Will it be Hate?
Will it be Trafficking?
Life is real.
Most live life with nervous energy.
Do you feel the atmosphere?
I fear my phone will ring and deliver the unbearable.
Expiration of your life because we look alike.
My fear is they will say you are missing without a trace.
Do you really want to share this journey or take my place?

Reminisce

Reminiscing,
Yearning for a time and place.
Back in the day,
Life was simple.
Joy in the world.
Children were free to enjoy life.
Laughing.
Dancing.
Playing.
Dreams superseded today's reality.
Carefree.
No worries.
Reminiscing about a time and place.
In my heart this was a peaceful place.
No lifeless being.
Only cookouts and parties.
What a dream...
No casualties of a world scorn by inadequate Healthcare, Poverty
or Stress.
Endless hurt.
Barely surviving, so all we do is work.
Praying for a time and place.
Reminiscing just to escape.

I Wish

Wish I could go back.
Turn back the hands of time.
Reminisce about the good times.
No sorrow or pain.
Family gatherings.
Sunshine.
Now it's only rain.
Loss.
The grief is real.
Sick and tired of the ashes-to-ashes and dust to dust.
Wishing to turn back the hands of time when it was all of us.
Jam packed under one roof.
Arguing.
Fighting.
Cooking.
Singing.
Love and games.
Those were the good days.
Forecast used to be sunshine.
Now it's overcast with rain.
Numb.
Wanna run.
Cannot move.
Wanna hide.
There's no space.
How do you cope when you cannot replace?
How do you accept what is,
When you want to touch what was?

One Life

One life.
Your life.
Live life.
Life, life, life.
Who cares what people think?
Everyone's shit stinks.
Do not compromise your integrity, goals, or dreams for man.
The Most High blessed you with life.
This is His land.
Live life.
Be purposeful.
This is your life.
Be blessed.
Live every minute.
Enjoy every breath.
Appreciate the journey.
Love it.
Cherish it.
Protect it.
Respect it.
Live your life with no regret.

Purpose

What is your Purpose?
Learning.
Working.
Teaching.
Preaching.
Dreaming.
Volunteering.
Family.
Sleeping.
Live life as He sees fit.
Live out your dreams.
Execute your plans.
Choose wisely.
Everyone has a path.
It's not easy.
Understand the reason for your existence.
No purpose is too tall when you are called.
A purpose worth living is a purpose worth fighting for.
Be willing to work wholeheartedly to do His will.
We have one life to get it right.
Are you ready for your call?
Are you living in your purpose?
When your time is up will you have fulfilled your purpose?

Earth Pains

The world is crumbling.
We're no longer operating on solid ground.
The foundation has been disturbed.
Earthquakes.
Volcanoes.
The earth is sending warning shocks.
Tornadoes.
Hurricanes.
Hear earth's pain.
The earth yearns to know its former self.
Years of abuse and neglect have shaken the world repeatedly.
The skies are gray.
The air is thickened from pollution.
The nurturers have turned their backs on earth.
Snowstorms.
Floods.
The earth is trying to tell its occupants something.

Lights Out

When the light is gone, how do you see?
When the flower has withered away, how do you survive?
When the well runs dry, how do you quench your thirst?
When the branch falls due to its weakened state, how do you extend your existence?
When the calls go unanswered, how do you go on?
When the source becomes lifeless, how do you stay informed?
When it ends, how do you begin?

Time Bomb

Tick!
Tick!
Tick!
The world has gone mad.
Bodies are dropping fast.
Explosions are nearby.
Hunger has increased globally.
The voiceless are completely stripped of their culture and heritage.
When lava spills, more people will be killed.
Most are numb but lack understanding.
People feel boxed in, unable to escape the new reality.
Who wins when every day is a new precedent for the unknown?
We are living in chaos.
The unholy become the holy.
The liars become credible.
The doctors become enabling drug pushers.
The world is a pressure cooker, ready to explode.
No one really knows how low this world will go.

The Times

It is hard to find happiness in a world thriving on destruction.
What should you do?
How do you cope?
It appears most have settled for a life with no hope.
Understand the times.
Are we living in the last days?
The good life seems like a distant memory.
Rumors of wars, natural disasters, disease, and hunger are our reality.
Are we living in a movie?
Are we living in the apocalypse?
Are we running out of time?
Be blessed and cherish your life.
We are living in the end times.

Life

Roses are pink.
Grass is green.
The ground is brown.
The sky is blue.
The clouds are gray.
Sometimes the forecast is a sunny day.
Sometimes tomorrow will bring a foggy haze.

The mornings are cold.
The afternoon produces a breeze.
A blizzard keeps people stagnate.
The wind blows in four directions.
Life keeps us guessing.

The journey is like a map.
We travel from point A to point B.
Don't give up on life.
Be determined.
Believe in your dreams.

FEELINGS

Heart of Gold

A dream on hold.
World so cold.
Can I live?
Can I live?
Are my dreams meaningless?
Heart of gold.
Dreams on hold.
Life.
This thing called life.
Choose wisely or pay the price.
Cost efficient.
Budget dreams.
Reality keeps me in arm's reach.
Living controlled.
Broken!
Dreams sold.
Postponed.
Procrastination.
Countless reevaluating.
Mind says it's patience.
Play your role!
Your time will come.
Just let it go.
Heart of gold.
Dreams on hold.
Life.
This life.
World so cold.

Emotional

Hot
Cold
Warm
Sunny
On time
Loud
Calm
Unpredictable
Wet
Slippery
Icy
Crazy
Bright
Moody
Fall
Winter
Storms
Spring
Blossom and Bloom
Summertime
Steamy
Fuego
Never ending
Feelings

Happy

Excited to see the smile that keeps the world at peace.
Delighted to be a part of the good things most people need.
Ecstatic about a chance to be the change that reaches our youth.
Elated to ensure that the teachings to the future are the truth.
Happy about the endless possibilities opening doors will bring.
Content to live in the moment because it was meant to be.
Optimistic about the chances to win.
Smiling with joy for happiness starts at the front door.

Gone

How can I express my pain?
Yearning to hear your voice.
Wishing to see your eyes full of life.
Hoping to feel your hugs again, as you hold me tight.
Wanting to hold on to every memory we cherished.
Needing to know that you are at peace.
Accepting the reality that you are no longer here with me.

Did I?

Did I forget your voice?
Searching for understanding.
Trying to reason with reality.
Coping with the unbelievable.
Dreaming for a memory of you.
Needing to have more time with you.
Knowing life must go on without you.

The Emotions that we Feel

Today is gray.
To be sad is to be blue.
Don't want to deal with reality.
Life is booby-trapped with casualties.
Sometimes, a break is needed from the nonstop drama life brings.
Cannot find time to decompress from all the stress.
The mind is wondering what's next.
The emotions that we feel in life are real.
Sometimes we do not understand why we feel the way we feel.
Sometimes we may feel down.
Often, life brings happiness.
There are extended periods of bliss.
Other times we may be upset.
At times, a frown is incorrigible.
The mind hurts as much as the physical and spiritual.
Sometimes we are emotionally and mentally drained.
Some moments we cannot explain.

Indifferent

Woke up one morning feeling indifferent.
How could this be?
My heart was emotionally detached.
I had fallen out of love with my daily routine.
Did my interest change overnight?
Was yesterday unbearable or more than I could handle?
Sometimes I toss and turn.
I'm up when I should be asleep.
Late when I should be on time.
This is becoming a never-ending situation.
However, it occurred to me the feeling is no longer mutual.
The action on both sides is one of displeasure.
My interest is indifferent.
I feel like running away from reality.
How could this be?
How do you learn to love your biggest investment when you have
fallen out of love?
Is it possible to start over after years of commitment?
The thought of something new gives me anxiety.
Separation issues are real, but settling for less is not a good
feeling.
Losing passion is a sign that something must change.
What do you do when you are indifferent about your daily
routine?

When It Hurts

Sometimes it is hard to fix what is broken.
If it is not meant to repair, why continue to care?
Investing time in the indifferent is like investing in a stock that has no chance of returns.
Continuing to bet on a dead-end situation is like betting on a baseball game when you've never watched or played the sport.
Saying goodbye today may hurt tomorrow but holding on to the inevitable leaves you with a sense of false hope, that will eventually hurt.
Carrying deadweight only makes life's trials heavier.
Sometimes the burden is unbearable but in time you cope.
Taking unnecessary chances on a lose-lose situation will only set you up for a lifetime of unnecessary pain.

Missing You

Not a day goes by, I do not cry.
Missing you dearly.
You are on my mind.
Missing your smile, jokes, love, and care.
Wishing to hug you.
Feel your spirit near.

The Saddest Day

The saddest day, I cried.
I prayed it was a lie.
I knew you were at peace, but I still had hope it was a dream.

The second saddest day, I screamed and cried.
I realized it wasn't a dream.
I had to gain the strength to say goodbye.
Shaking and weak, I couldn't believe it.
I felt your presence in the air.
My heart was filled with love.
My grandmother was no longer physically here.
She gained her wings.
Mother Earth is resting peacefully.

LOVE

Love

I love to love.
Live to love.
Want to love.
Need to love.
Love, love, love.
Hope to love.
Feel your love.
See your love.
Believe in your love.
Love, love, love.
Love.

What a Feeling?

Love
What a feeling?
Happy
Sad
Lustful
Sensual
Spiritual
Connection
Mesmerizing
Addictive
Battle tested
Angry
Journey
Up and down
Hot and cold
Bold
Old
Sold
Stolen
Robbed
Scary
In vain
Emotional
War zone
Corrupt
Politically correct
Prideful
Boastful
Joyous memories
Forgetful
Regretful
Taken for granted
Some timey
Funkier than breath
Stinky stench
Emotional roller-coaster
Love
What a feeling?

Unconditional

Jump for joy.
Don't be coy.
I see it in your eyes.
Love never dies.
So calm, like a breeze.
Cherish and engulf this beautiful journey.
I will be there when the well runs dry.
Quench your thirst with hope and motivation.
Lift you up when you stumble.
Loosen the grip when life seems tense.
Look you in your eyes with honesty and no judgement.
Cheer you on when you close the deal.
Hold you in my arms when you are in a world full of pain.
Provide the keys when doors are locked.
Provide clarity in a world cloudier than a foggy day.
Please return the favor, you are on the clock.

Deserve

You deserve to be loved.
You deserve to be loved without conditions.
You deserve the best.
You deserve to be stress free.
You deserve to be heard.
You deserve to have peace.
You deserve to feel safe when you walk the streets.
You deserve to be praised for your hard work.
You deserve to be one with your queen.
You deserve to be treated like a king.

Worthy

Understand your worth.
You are enough.
Value yourself to not lay down with any man.
You are worthy to be treated as a queen.
You are worthy of being able to rest in your femininity.
You are worthy of unconditional love.
You are worthy of peace.
You are worthy of being understood.
You are worthy of protection.
You are worthy of having a helping hand.
You are worthy of your king.

Show Me

It's not enough for you to tell me how you feel.
Your actions speak to my inner soul.
When you hold me close, I feel consoled.
Knock! Knock!
Open up, let your guard down, and let me in.
Trust me with your heart.
Us together is a win.
Sometimes, I need to know where we stand.
At times, I yearn to hear those words, "I love you."
Today, I yearn for you to show me just how much your love is true.

A Mother's Love

A Mother's love is unmatched.
Sleepless nights, just to make sure her little ones are alright.
Healing hands.
Strength beyond understanding.
A Mother's love — oh, what a beautiful feeling.
She works countless hours to ensure her children have everything they need.
Willing to go toe to toe with the world to defend, fight, or stand up for her child.
Do not test the will and determination of Mama.
A Mother's love — oh, what a beautiful feeling.
Mother represents,
Safety.
Security.
Love.
Wisdom.
Hope.
Mama love.
Mama love.
You are a blessing from above.
Willing to sacrifice her wellbeing for her youth.
Mom may seem stern, but she sees the bigger picture.
Mother sees your future and wants the best for you.
She's trying to prepare you for the realities in life.
The world is cold.
Mama has the words to uplift your spirit.
Mother has a heart of gold.
Sacrifices her me time to love on her babies.
A Mother's love — oh, what a beautiful feeling.
Mother represents,
Compassion.
Selfless.
Special.
Giving.

Kind.
Mama love.
Mama love.
Ain't no Mama like mine, but I'm sure yours is as special as mine.
Love, Respect, Cherish, and Honor your Mother.

Cost

The cost of love is priceless.

Opening up and being vulnerable to love someone is risky.

Not everyone has good intentions and sometimes intentions intend to leave you broken.

The cost of love can amount to a life filled with heartache or a life filled with genuine love and romance because sometimes, the risk to love pays off.

The price to love is expensive but worth the sweaty palms and heart palpitations.

Though costly, the feeling of love is worth every trial and all the endless good moments.

There's nothing too expensive when you've found your better half.

Pieces of the Puzzle

Picking up the pieces of love loss hurts.

The pain feels never-ending.

Time stops and every second feels like forever.

The days move slowly.

The nights feel lonely.

The summers are colder than winter.

Winter feels like a hot summer day.

Often, we try to forget the pain by moving forward without dealing with the pain, but the reality of a failed relationship remains untamed.

Though it may seem like a puzzle missing pieces, deal with love loss.

Take the proper time to heal and pick up your missing pieces.

To be complete, you must first start with the first piece.

To Love

The chance to love is a blessing.
The experience of love can be breath taking.
Once you are touched by love, cherish every moment.
Be willing to go to war for the love given to you from above.
To love is to live.
To love is to thrive.
To love is to cry.
To love is to realize true love never dies.

INSPIRATION

Stop

Stop fighting the inevitable.
Stop holding back.
You are better than the image you portray.
Stop speaking your demise into existence.
Stop hating and erasing your own existence.
Stop being the reason they draw sketches on the ground at crime scenes.
Stop living a life of greed.
Stop holding your head down walking through life with a frown.
Stop trying to rewrite, alter, or stall fate.
Stop moving in life with regret and hate.

Stand Tall

Stand tall.
Be proud of who you are.
No matter where you are in life, you have come far.
It's not easy being you but stay true.
Live your life.
Love and appreciate you.
Remember to guide, respect, and trust your judgement.
Life can be challenging.
Heartache.
Cold.
Lonely.
Hold on.
Have hope.
Stand tall.
We all fall.
It's not easy.
It won't be perfect.
But in the end, trust and believe, it will be worth it.

Dreams

There is nothing wrong with having dreams.
Hope.
Inspiration.
Motivation.
Determination.
Take your time.
Good things come to those who are patient.
Your dreams can become your reality.
Struggling is a part of life.
Stumbling builds character.
Endure.
Have faith.
Be your biggest investor.
Speak it into existence.
And understand dreams can be real if you believe in it.

Appreciation

Life is constantly changing. Trials may seem never-ending. Dreams may seem far away. Loved ones resting may seem like a distant memory. Losses may feel like your only accomplishment.

Every breath you take is a blessing. Although lessons in life are tough, He won't put you through more than you can endure. The faithful servant will always rise even when it seems like your only chance of surviving is to fall. Every day is another chance to be great. A home to rest your head is security. A plate to eat means nourishment. Heat and clothing bring warmth.

The bad news is long gone. The losses are now constant wins. Life is healthy. Healing is never-ending. Today is a better day. You are in a better place. You are winning. Don't take life for granted. Live life as if it is ending.

Today

Today is your day.
A blessing in disguise.
An opportunity to mend yesterday's infractions.
The chance to be the best version of yourself.
See your worth.
Understand your value in every aspect of your life.
Do not cheat yourself by settling for less.
You are amazing and deserve the best.

Don't let it get away

Never give up on yourself.
Though you may have doubts, never lose sight of your goals.
We all have dreams.
Dreams can be your reality.
Believe in yourself.
Understand that it may not work the first time but continue to try and give your best.
The chances you never take today are the regrets you'll have tomorrow.

Sometimes

Sometimes, when it no longer feels right, it's no good.
We give so much time and effort to the things that leave us empty inside.
Sometimes, we prolong the inevitable, hoping things will improve but they never do.
Who told you to settle?
Who told you to devalue your worth?
Who said it was ok to accept less than great?
Understand, just how valuable you are.
Stop settling for the things that prevent you from reaching your potential.
Overworking doesn't necessarily equate to success.
You are the best, stop accepting less.
You are a commodity.
There can only be one you.
Everything may appear to be great.
Imagine spending 40 years faking it to make it, just to barely get by.
Boss up.
Make sure your success feels good inside.

Family

We are family. Some may be distant. Some may be near. Cousins from different tribes, but I feel the unity amongst us. When I say Sis, it's always LOVE. When I call you my brother, just know that I CARE. We come from the same struggle. Motivated and inspired by the same fears. We all yearn and long for the best for our people. We come in different shades, but the resemblance is remarkable. When you hurt, I CRY. When you win, I WIN. When you struggle, I'm right by your side. We are forever tied. Family ties. I love you, blessed tribe.

Fallen

In life, we all have fallen; sometimes our confidence is shaken.
Every day is a new day, another day filled with tests.
Sometimes we feel hopeless in a world filled with different stressors.
No matter how many times you fall, look at a new day as a better day.
Tomorrow is a fresh start, a new blessing for you to grow and learn a new lesson.
No matter how many times you stumble or fail, do not get discouraged or look back.
Have faith, tomorrow will be your day.

Fight, Fight, Fight

We must be motivated to acquire the things we desire.
Hard work is important.
Patience is invaluable.
Sometimes it may not go your way.
Fight, fight, fight.
Don't give up on your dreams.
Plan accordingly.
Goals are important.
Time management is a key component to achieve your goals.
Fight, fight, fight.
There's nothing wrong with having faith and believing in yourself.
You are not talentless.
Take a chance on yourself.
You are worth the risk.
Your best investment is to invest in yourself.
There will be setbacks and sometimes the outcome may be unfavorable.
Never give up.
Continue to walk steadily towards your goals.
Fight, fight, fight.
The chances you don't take while be the regret you cannot escape.

WOKE

Change

Change!
Dreaming of change.
Hard to imagine living this life.
Free but in bondage by your laws.
Reparations you feel will settle Americas flaws.

Change!
Dreaming of change.
Last chance to get it right.
Equality.
We will fight for our rights, to be treated as humans.
Inhale fresh air.
Drive around without being profiled.
Live with no fear.
The car pulled over; we made it home.
No lifeless bodies.
No tears.

Change!
Dreaming of change.
Woke as fuck.
Licking shots, no hope.
No need to duck.
Stuck facing reality of hopeless dreams.
Want change!
Most won't survive this life.
Such a pain.
Change.
Dreaming of change.

Unbelievable

Struggling to live life.
The middle class is unclassified.
The poor will not survive.
Families are hurting, begging for assistance.
Food banks needing loans.
Warning.
Warning.
Danger zone.
Hopelessness.
The rich are filthy rich.
Unbelievable decisions made by those with deep pockets and fat
bellies.
How could they understand?
How could they make sound decisions on behalf of the working
man?
They are incapable of understanding.
They lack the knowledge to speak.
Misinformed.
Out of touch.
Emotionally dead.
Their ignorance is a choice.
Naively, the people voted you as their voice.
It is unfortunate you lack humility and understanding.
The elected is incapable of relating to its constituents.
Unqualified to lead and uplift the people.
The aroma of corruption is in the air.
The mistrust in this land is reality.
America torn down by man.
Most cannot understand, so they settle for the lesser of evil.
Evil is evil.
Neither one will help the people.
We are entering dangerous times.
Warning.
Warning.
America is Falling.

Tired

No value.
Understand my people.
We are better.
Deserve better.
Unintentional generations of hate passed down.
Understand we cannot sustain life on earth putting each other in the ground.
Battling for respect, acceptance, and equality from the world.
Some look at us and laugh.
They call us weak.
Don't respect us when we speak.
We look at each other and don't see value in each other.
My Brothers,
Love each other.
Keep us safe from this cruel world.
Appreciate and value your women.
It's a tough world, we are repeating our ancestor's history.
Field slave, house slave. It's called "divide and conquer."
The hate is so real we rape, murder, rob and kill.
Will we be extinct as a people?
We are the people.
Love and honor your fathers and mothers.
Put the guns down and pick up your brothers.
Listen to each other because we understand each other's pain.
Stop living life in vain.
We should want our community to win.
Cheer each other on.
Stand as one on solid ground before the light burns out.
Good night.

World Unfamiliar

Woke up in a different place.
World unfamiliar.
Economic crisis.
Millions starving.
Death rate unacceptable.
Job losses.
Stressed beyond repair.
Distant fears are near.
Leaders do not care.
Walking on eggshells.
Contaminated air.
The world we've known is no longer here.

Wonder Why

Why?
How dare you question why?
Since conception they had a target on their backs.
All because they are so called Black.
Stopped, frisked, and thrown to the ground.
Don't move or make a sound unless you want to be buried in the ground.
Your life is on the line because you fit their description.
Generations of profiling and unjust treatment.
Innocence stolen and snatched away.
Illegal choke holds are the *code*.
Stop and listen.
Toy guns are manufactured and authorized for child's play, but when you look a certain way,
It's a right to justify an early grave.

Pain

The pain runs deep.
Sick and tired of seeing RIP.
Can't eat.
Toss and turn.
My skin color seems to burn a hole through the soulless.
Can't walk.
Can't work.
Can't think.
Can't exist.
While the "so called Black man" is often dealt a losing hand.
Separated from our identity.
Sleepless nights wondering: *who we are?*
Searching for understanding.
Asking questions but the government isn't answering.
Public enemy #1 over who we could be.
Cursed from birth but our hair, skin, and soul bring vibrant life, a beautiful energy.
We may fight and argue with each other, but do not have to share the same name to understand each other's pain.
My brother identifies with your brother.
My mother looks like your mother.
Our grandparents walked similar paths.
Shared stories with the youth about our ancestor's pain.
Picking cotton, nurturing master and misses seed.
The hatred and greed have produced a life of luxury.
Wake up my people.
Get your head in the game.
Remember your true name.
His Story.
His Will.
Repent.
Give your life to HIM or continue to suffer in pain.

Let My People Go

Let my people go.
Shackles.
Mentally.
Physically.
Spiritually.
Financially.
Culturally.

Let my people go.
Unite as one.
Feared as one unit.
There is strength in numbers.
Imagine the mighty force our family could be.
Let's get our house in order.
Father.
Mother.
Son.
Daughter.
Organize.
Law and order.

Let my people go.
So, we can live a life of:
Hope.
Love.
Respect.
Dignity.
Pride.
Wanna see my community thrive without the oppressor's lie.

I See You

Young man, please understand the life you are leading ain't it.
Robbing.
Stealing.
Killing.
This cannot be your life.
When you pull the trigger, it's an act of self-hatred.
You claim, he's not your brother, he's just another nigga.
And, every trigger that you pull is self-genocide against your own people.
Young man, I see the hope in you.
Turn from the hatred in your heart.
Stop devaluing yourself by killing your brother.
Look at the bigger picture.
You were chosen for a better purpose.
His life is worth it.
Stop the violence.
Today be great.
Choose life.
Choose hope.
Choose you.
Choose to be the change they said you could not be.
When you think of your brother, speak life into his inner being.
Speak love.
Speak Hope.
Speak the Truth.
Your actions have aided in our people not winning.
There is no hope for the future until you spare the future.
Life!
Young man do not treat tonight like another ordinary night.
See life because I see you.

What Matters?

Is it worldly things?
Everything that glitters ain't gold.
But you chose to sell your soul.
Turn your back on your community.
Rob, kill, and steal just for thrills.
Promote self-hate and genocide to the youth.

What matters?

Do you care to know the truth?
So, you think drugs and sex is the ultimate appeal.
Burning internally.
Can't stand the reflection in the rear.
Hurting inside.
Is it pride?
You wear your mask well.
Glorifying gangs and jail when you never touched a cell.
Condemned the everyday working man because he wasn't cool.
Trying to hustle on the corner, young brother that ain't you.

What matters?

Is it glorifying whoredom?
Half-naked.
Raunchy stench.
Selling slut dreams to our teens.
They say it's for the culture.
Hoes and BMs is our goals.
We were once Queens; we sold our crowns for stilettos and silver poles.

What matters?

Is it the standards we were given?

The current state or the continued self-hate.
The self-genocide, we should be fighting for our lives.
We are slowly dying.
Get a grip.
Take back your soul.
Remember who you are.
Let the world know, they can no longer promote, buy, or invest in our generational destruction.

It takes a Tribe.

We need the tribe more than ever.
We are slowly dying as a community.
Our community lacks loyalty.
Parents encourage, applaud, and praise the self-destruction of our youth.
Who the hell raised you?
You know you had to be home before the streetlights came on.
You couldn't listen to that song.
Your eyes were covered by the deceptive lights on the screen.
It all seems like a dream, but this is our reality.
Truth be told, at the rate we are going it will be hard for us to sustain longevity.
No hope for our future.
Our youth is our future.
Drugs, violence and oversexualization of our youth is the new norm.
We were formed from Greatness.
Self-destruction and self-hate get worse from generation to generation.
We are a fractured people.
We are becoming an incorrigible nation.
It is painful to see.
We are failing our ancestors.
Let's take it back.
See back in the day, accountability was the tribe.
The struggle was real, but the tribe was there.
Friends were brothers.
We shared grandmothers.
Sisters rejoiced at the success of her fellow sisters.
Checks and balances were a part of our nation.
The tribe is needed.
The tribe is our only hope.

REFLECTIONS (BONUS)

Letter of Reflections

Let us Reflect on Life which causes us to have Feelings based on our encounters and experiences. Sometimes, we invite people into our lives which causes us to experience what we perceive as Love. At times, temporary setbacks, and the people we cross paths with is the Inspiration we need to motivate ourselves or others to reach their potential. Most often, the world we never knew, the world we use to know, the current state of the world or the world that's yet to come will have you Woke. Although your feelings are your feelings, be responsible, understanding, and respectful. Stay blessed.

The World

the world is dependent on its occupants
temporary tenants

paying fees on top of fees
to fill the bellies of thieves

while the poor work countless hours, barely surviving
now pushed out on the streets

middle class is under the allusion that the elected is who you
should be choosing
but
when will you see it was all in the name of greed

Pressure

Mind racing.
Decisions, decisions, decisions.
Better choose wisely.
Bad decisions.
Wrong choices.
Procrastination.
Backing out.
Searching and finding reasons to not make a move.
So much pressure.
One wrong move can lead to a life of heartache and pain.
The stress of so much pressure infiltrates the brain.
Mind racing.
Heart skipping beats.
Parched with no words, I cannot speak.

Temporary Love

Sometimes what we think is Love, simply is not love. If you must question it maybe it isn't meant. Sure, we all reflect and make changes for the betterment of our own well-being and for our better half; however, your better half should inspire you to be better. Uplift you with words and actions of encouragement. What they say should always match what they do. When they say, I love you understand when it is true. Some use love because they truly love you. Others use love because they truly need you. Is it a need that satisfies love or is it the want that makes us blind to reality? Either way let no man lead you astray. If the love is real there will be no conditions or restrictions. Understand and listen, most will tell you where they lie. The lie may part from their lips. The lie may come in the form of a kiss. The lie may come in the form of cash. The lie may come in the form of giving ass. What we perceive as love isn't love, it's the distortion of love. Often, we think love is perfect but that type of love is fake. It's imperfect but perfect between the two. Understand which is you. Temporary love wasn't temporary, it simply wasn't true.

A Little Motivation

A little motivation is all we need to be inspired to achieve our dreams. A little bit of motivation is all it takes to make an inspired person want to be great. Never give up on your dreams, we all fall short daily because the burdens we carry are too much to lift on our own. Position yourself in spaces with people who truly appreciate and love who you are and who you will ultimately be. The progress you make today is the set up for the best version of yourself tomorrow. So, be motivated by the ones who truly have good intentions for you. It's okay, today, to not be okay but don't allow today's troubles or setbacks to be a lifetime of burdens. Take a load off and don't carry the burden forever.

Boarded up doors

Shattered dreams.
Broken glass on the streets.
Battling for survival.
Hearts on the ground.
Soul's loss.
Visually trying to see tomorrow.
Until further notice, we will be drowning out our sorrows.
Hoping to see daylight.
Praying to breathe new life.
Willing to fight for equality.
Most people are living in poverty.
While the elite are mentally at peace.
Crime rates continue to increase.
They no longer advocate for world peace.
Most people are exempt from true opportunities.
All we can do is pray and hope for a better day.
We all want to truly be free.
Taxation.
Criminalization.
Imprisonment
Redlining.
Fighting for a livable wage, we want to be compensated properly.
We protest to increase or eliminate the minimum wage, but the corporation must get paid.
So, we seek affordable Healthcare, so we can get adequate care.
We understand that you do not care.
Before you walk away, listen, and consider our struggle.

Shades of Emotions

Acknowledgements

I want to thank The Most High for giving me the courage and blessing me with the ability to share my poetry with the world.

In addition, I want to thank my family and friends for always being supportive.

Furthermore, I want to thank my editor for always doing a wonderful job and making sense of my words. Many thanks to my graphic designer, you always go above and beyond to format my books and create beautiful covers.

ALSO, BY TIKIA CLEMENT

COMING SOON FROM

TIKIA CLEMENT

Children's Book

Dreams Can Be Real Series. Career Day with Olivia

Poetry Book
The Decalogue